Jesus Speaks to Me About EASTER

BY ANGELA M. BURRIN • ILLUSTRATED BY MARIA CRISTINA LO CASCIO

The Death of Jesus

"I am the Resurrection and the Life."
John 11:25

Welcome to this book about Easter! When you think about Easter, do you picture Easter eggs, baby chicks, and spring flowers? These are symbols of new life. Now I want to tell you stories about this new life—one that my heavenly Father and I want you to live with us each day.

My Father always wanted his sons and daughters to have hearts that loved him and other people. But after Adam and Eve disobeyed him in the Garden of Eden, his children didn't always choose what was right.

So my Father sent me from heaven to earth to put things right. I loved teaching the crowds. The miracles I did showed the people how much their heavenly Father loved them.

But not everyone liked what I said and did. I had enemies who plotted to kill me. Soldiers arrested me in the Garden of Gethsemane. One of them pushed a crown of thorns into my head. Others gave me a heavy cross to carry up the hill of Calvary.

As I hung on the cross, I knew that I was taking on the punishment for everyone's sins. But I also knew that three days after my death, I would rise to new life!

Jesus, the crucifix reminds me how much you love me.
Right now I want to thank you for dying for all of my sins.

The Resurrection of Jesus

MARY MAGDALENE SAID, "I HAVE SEEN THE LORD."
John 20:18

Easter Sunday is the day I rose from the dead. I'm alive! My body is changed—I now have a glorified body that will live forever. And the gates of heaven are now open!

Mary Magdalene was the first person to see me. Early in the morning she had come to the tomb to anoint my body with perfumed oils. But what do you think she saw? The big stone in front of my tomb had been rolled away. The tomb was empty! Two angels were sitting where my body had been. When they asked Mary why she was crying, she said, "Because someone has stolen Jesus' body."

I stood behind Mary and asked, "Why are you crying?" She thought I was the gardener. Mary said, "Someone has taken Jesus. If you did it, tell me where you have put him. I will go to him there."

When I said her name, "Mary," she knew it was me. Oh, Mary was so happy! She wanted to keep holding onto me. But I said, "Mary, go and tell my other friends that I've risen from the dead." Mary ran and told my disciples, "Jesus is alive. I've seen him!"

Jesus, I'm so happy that you are alive!
I invite you to come into my heart. Please be my best friend.

On the Road to Emmaus

"THEIR EYES WERE OPENED AND THEY RECOGNIZED HIM."
Luke 24:31

On Easter Sunday I also appeared to two of my disciples. They were walking to Emmaus. "Why did Jesus have to die?" they asked each other.

When I joined them, they didn't recognize me. They began telling me, "A man named Jesus who did mighty deeds was crucified. And now some of his friends are saying he is alive. How can that be?"

As we walked along the road, I explained what Moses and the prophets had written about me in the Scriptures. When we arrived in Emmaus, my two friends said, "Stay and eat with us." During the meal, I took a piece of bread, thanked my Father, broke it, and gave it to them. All of a sudden they recognized me, but immediately I disappeared! They said to each other, "Weren't our hearts burning as Jesus spoke to us?"

Wasn't it wonderful how my two friends recognized me in the Scriptures and in the blessed bread? It can be the same for you, too, when you read the Bible and receive me in the Eucharist at Mass. In these ways our friendship will grow.

Jesus, I want our friendship to grow.
I will read a story about you in my Bible every day
and receive you often in the Eucharist.

Breakfast with Jesus

"BRING SOME OF THE FISH YOU HAVE JUST CAUGHT."
John 21:10

One evening not long after my resurrection, Peter and some of his friends went fishing. From the shore I called out, "Have you caught any fish?" They said, "No," so I told them, "Throw your net over the other side of the boat." Immediately their net was filled with fish—so many fish that the net nearly tore!

That's when Peter recognized me. "It's Jesus!" he said as he jumped into the water. On the beach I had started a charcoal fire. "Come and have breakfast," I said to them, and we cooked some of the fish. How good it tasted!

While we were eating, I asked Peter three times if he loved me. Three times he replied, "Yes, Jesus, I love you." Three times I said, "Feed my sheep."

What did I mean by that? You'll see as you read the other stories in this book! Just as I helped Peter catch fish, I helped him to tell people the truth about me. I also chose Peter to become the first pope.

Do you know someone who is "feeding my sheep"? Talk with your parents about that person. Perhaps you could read about a saint who told others about my love.

Jesus, today I want to tell someone about you.
Bless the Pope, priests, and all those who share the good news about Easter.

The Ascension

"AND REMEMBER, I AM WITH YOU ALWAYS."
Matthew 28:20

Do you have a photo of the day you received the Sacrament of Baptism? On that special day, you became a member of your heavenly Father's family of love. The Holy Spirit placed the seed of my new life within you!

For forty days after Easter, I appeared to my disciples. I loved talking about the new life that I died on the cross to give everyone. "In a few days, you will be baptized with the Holy Spirit," I promised them. "And remember, I am with you always."

Then the day arrived for me to return to my Father. I took my friends to the Mount of Olives, and after blessing them, I ascended into heaven. They stood watching me until clouds hid me from their sight. Now I am seated at the right hand of my Father in his kingdom.

Just like my disciples, you cannot see me with your eyes. But don't forget: I am with you always! If you are at home, at school, or playing with your friends, I am with you. I know what you need. You are my special friend.

Jesus, thank you for always being with me!
In my morning and night prayers,
I will say, "My heavenly Father loves me very much."

The Feast of Pentecost

"ALL OF THEM WERE FILLED WITH THE HOLY SPIRIT."

Acts 2:4

Do you know what happened ten days after my ascension? My heavenly Father sent the Holy Spirit!

I had told my disciples and Mary, my mother, to wait in the Upper Room in Jerusalem. Because they were afraid, they had locked the doors. Suddenly they heard a loud noise like a rushing wind. Then flames of fire appeared over everyone's head. "It's the Holy Spirit!" they said. "Jesus has kept his promise!"

The Holy Spirit does amazing things in people's lives! Suddenly my disciples were very brave. They ran into the streets, telling the people about me. Jerusalem was full of Jews from different countries celebrating the yearly feast of Pentecost. The Holy Spirit helped the disciples speak in foreign languages so that everyone could understand them. The people were so surprised!

Peter told the crowds, "Jesus was sent to save us from our sins. You put him to death on a cross. But now he is alive. We've seen him!" The people said, "What can we do?" Peter replied, "Ask your heavenly Father to forgive your sins and fill you with the power of the Holy Spirit."

Holy Spirit, at bedtime, show me where I have sinned that day
and help me to say a good Act of Contrition.

The Early Christian Community

"They broke bread in their homes and ate together."
Acts 2:46

Pentecost was very special. That day about three thousand people were baptized. Now, filled with the Holy Spirit, all these people were able to live the new life.

And this is how the early Christians lived. People came together in little groups or communities. They sang and praised God and ate their meals together. During the meal, bread was blessed, broken, and given to everyone, in memory of what I did at my Last Supper.

They also shared what they owned. When a family didn't have enough food, they said, "Here is something to eat." If they were unkind to someone, they said, "Please forgive me." That showed that they had new life in their hearts.

People saw how the early Christians loved one another. Often they would ask, "Why are you so happy, kind, and generous?" They would answer, "It's because the Holy Spirit lives inside of us. He is our helper." Because of their witness, many others accepted Jesus as their Lord and Savior. They, too, were baptized in the Holy Spirit and began living the new life. And so my church grew and grew.

You, too, are a member of a community—your parish family.

Holy Spirit, I'm so thankful that you are my helper.
Show me how I can help someone in my family or parish.

Signs and Wonders

Peter prayed, "Tabitha, get up!"
Acts 9:40

Living the new life was an adventure for Peter and my disciples. They left their homes and traveled to many different towns and cities. They knew the Holy Spirit would show them where to go!

One day two men ran up to Peter and said, "Come quickly! A kind woman named Tabitha had been sick, but now she's died."

So Peter went with them to the nearby town of Joppa where Tabitha lived. He went upstairs to her room. Tabitha's family and friends were around her, crying and comforting each other. The widows told Peter, "Look at the clothes Tabitha made for us. She used the gifts God gave her to help us."

Peter said, "Everyone, please leave the room." He knelt down and prayed that the Holy Spirit would work a miracle through him. "Tabitha, get up." And a miracle happened! Tabitha opened her eyes and sat up. Peter took Tabitha's hand and helped her to stand up.

"Tabitha is alive," everyone cried out. Soon lots of people in Joppa heard about this miracle. And guess what? Many others believed in me and began to live the new life too!

Holy Spirit, thank you for the gift of healing.
Help me to remember to pray for sick people when I'm at Mass.

The Stoning of Stephen

THEY DRAGGED STEPHEN OUTSIDE OF THE CITY AND BEGAN TO STONE HIM.

Acts 7:58

A flashing red light means "Warning, warning!" I warned my special friends that some of them would suffer and die because they loved me and told others about me. But that didn't stop them! Let me tell you about Stephen. He was the first martyr.

Stephen was filled with my Holy Spirit and did miracles in my name. He loved telling people about my Father's kingdom and why I came from heaven to earth. Some of the religious leaders didn't want to hear the truths that Stephen was speaking. "You are wrong!" they shouted, and they began to argue with him. But the Holy Spirit gave Stephen courage and the right words to answer their questions.

One day the leaders got so angry with Stephen that they rushed toward him and dragged him outside of the city. Then they picked up stones and began throwing them at him.

While they were stoning him, Stephen prayed, "Jesus, receive my spirit." He fell on his knees and asked my Father to forgive them: "Lord, do not hold this sin against them." Then Stephen died and joined me in heaven.

Holy Spirit, I want to be forgiving like Stephen.
As I pray an Our Father, remind me of anyone I need to forgive.

Philip's Ride in a Chariot

PHILIP PROCLAIMED THE GOOD NEWS ABOUT JESUS.
Acts 8:35

Are you ready for another exciting story? This one is about a man named Philip. He had heard what happened on Easter Sunday and became one of my followers. Now Philip was an obedient man. When an angel told him, "Go south on the desert road," he did it immediately.

On that road he heard a chariot coming. In it was an important person in charge of money for the queen of Ethiopia. The Holy Spirit gave Philip another instruction: "Go to that chariot." The Ethiopian man was reading the Book of Isaiah. Philip asked, "Do you understand what you are reading?" The Ethiopian answered, "How can I unless someone explains it to me? Tell me, who is the prophet Isaiah talking about, himself or someone else?"

Philip got into the chariot, saying, "I will tell you everything about Jesus." When they saw some water, the Ethiopian asked Philip, "Will you baptize me in the name of Jesus?" Together they went into the water.

After coming out of the water, the Holy Spirit suddenly took Philip away. The Ethiopian never saw him again. But because of Philip's obedience, the Ethiopian's life had been changed forever. He had received new life!

Jesus, sometimes it is hard for me to be obedient.
Help me listen to my parents and be obedient to them.

Jesus Meets Paul

"I AM JESUS. YOU ARE HURTING ME."
Acts 9:5

I always loved Paul. But he didn't always know me or love me. Keep reading!

Paul, who was also called Saul, was a Pharisee. He was always careful to obey the Law. He knew that a Messiah would come. But when he heard people saying, "Jesus is the Messiah," he became very worried. "He's not the Messiah," he said. "I must go to Damascus and find all the believers of Jesus. I'll arrest them and put them in prison."

I didn't want Paul to be my enemy. As he was traveling to Damascus, I sent a flashing light that knocked him down. I said, "Saul, Saul, why are you persecuting me?' Saul was frightened and said, "Who are you, Lord?" I replied, "I am Jesus. You are persecuting me."

When Saul got up from the ground, he was blind. Some men led him to Damascus. There a man named Ananias told him, "Saul, Jesus has chosen you to tell others about him."

That day Paul became my friend. After Ananias prayed with him, he could see again! My Father would use Paul to share the good news with people all over the world.

Jesus, it must make you sad that many people still don't know you or love you.
I will pray a decade of the rosary, asking Mary to intercede for them.

Peter's Amazing Dream

"They have received the Holy Spirit, just like we have."
Acts 10:47

At first my disciples told only people who were Jewish about me and what had happened on Easter Sunday. But that was about to change.

There was a Roman centurion named Cornelius who was not Jewish. One day in a dream, an angel told him, "Ask a man named Peter, who is in Joppa, to come visit you." So Cornelius sent three men to find Peter.

At the same time, Peter was praying on the roof of a house in Joppa. He also had a dream. He saw a sheet being lowered from heaven full of unclean animals, reptiles, and birds. A voice said, "Eat these animals." Peter, who always kept the Jewish food laws, said, "No, I can't do that!" The voice replied, "Do not call unclean anything that God has made clean." Then the voice said, "Three men are looking for you. Go with them."

A crowd was waiting for Peter when he arrived at Cornelius' house. Suddenly Peter understood his dream. "Oh, my Father wants everyone, not just Jews, to know about Jesus." As Peter was telling them the good news, the Holy Spirit filled the hearts of everyone! Cornelius and his family and friends were baptized, and they, too, began to live the new life.

Jesus, help me to be friends with everyone, even those who are different from me.

Paul Is Shipwrecked

My apostle Paul wasn't popular with everyone. Several times he was put in prison. One time, guarded by a Roman centurion, he was put on a ship headed for the important city of Rome.

Not long after the ship left the harbor, there was a bad storm, and the winds became very strong. For days huge waves crashed against the ship. Everyone was terrified. "We are going to drown," they cried. But Paul said, "An angel of God has told me that we will be shipwrecked but that no one will die."

The next morning, the winds calmed down and the ship got stuck on a sandbar. Everyone jumped into the water and got safely to the shore. After that adventure, Paul went into the nearby towns and told everyone, "Jesus is alive."

Well, that's my last story—but the story of Easter continues. And you're part of the story! The Holy Spirit wants to help you live my new life every day—by spending time with me, by being kind and generous, by forgiving others, and by telling others about me. Listen to the Holy Spirit and do what he says. And remember, I'm alive, I love you, and I'm always with you.

Jesus, I love you. I'm so happy you're alive!
Thank you for teaching me about Easter.

Published in 2012 in the U.S. and Canada by
The Word Among Us Press
7115 Guilford Road
Frederick, Maryland
www.wau.org

ISBN: 978-1-59325-220-5

Publishing Director: Annette Reynolds
Art Director: Gerald Rogers
Pre-production: Krystyna Kowalska Hewitt
Production: John Laister

Printed and bound in Malaysia
September 2012